MR. BUG'S PHONICS

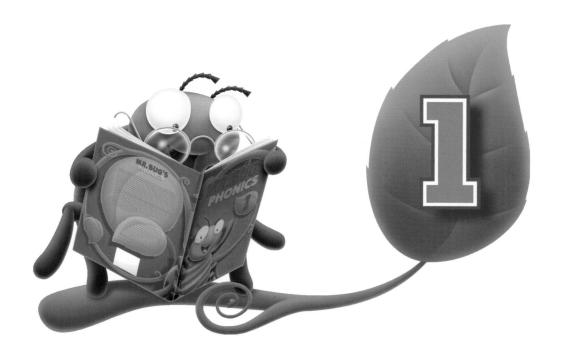

1

by
Catherine Yang Eisele
Richmond Hsieh

OXFORD UNIVERSITY PRESS

Oxford University Press
198 Madison Avenue
New York, Ny 10016 USA

Great Clarendon Street
Oxford OX2 6DP England

Oxford New York
Auckland Bangkok Buenos Aires Cape Town Chennai
Dar es Salaam Delhi Hong Kong Istanbul Karachi Kolkata
Kuala Lumpur Madrid Melbourne Mexico City Mumbai
Nairobi São Paulo Shanghai Singapore Taipei Tokyo Toronto

with an associated company in Berlin

OXFORD is a trademark of Oxford University Press

ISBN 0-19-435252-8

Editorial Manager: Shelagh Speers
Senior Editor: Sherri Arbogast
Elementary Design Manager: Doris Chen
Production Editor: Joseph McGasko
Production Manager: Abram Hall

Design and Production: Carrie Hamilton/Bill SMITH STUDIO
Mr. Bug Illustrations: Bernard Adnet
Story Illustrations: Michele Noiset
Page Illustrations: Patrick Girouard, Patti Goodnow, N. Jo, Ronnie Shipman

Cover Design: Carrie Hamilton/Bill SMITH STUDIO
Cover Illustration by Bernard Adnet

Printing (last digit): 10 9

Printed in China

Contents

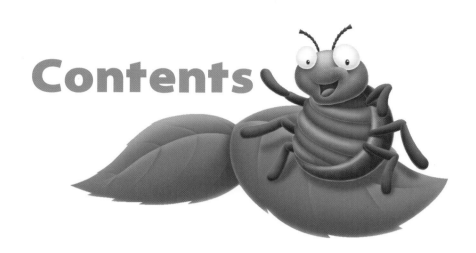

Unit 1	Aa, Bb, Cc	2
Unit 2	Dd, Ee, Ff	10
Unit 3	Gg, Hh, Ii	18
Unit 4	Jj, Kk, Ll	26
Unit 5	Mm, Nn, Oo	34
Unit 6	Pp, Qq, Rr	42
Unit 7	Ss, Tt, Uu	50
Unit 8	Vv, Ww, Xx	58
Unit 9	Yy, Zz	66
Review Song		73
Vocabulary Review		74

Story Time

Listen and point.

New Words

Listen to the chant. Then find the stickers.

Aa

Find another **a** word.

Bb

Find another **b** word.

Cc

Find another **c** word.

Now say the chant!

4

Aa Practice

Look and do.

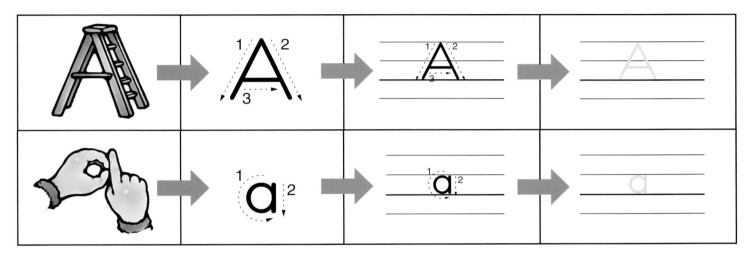

Write and say.

A A

a a

Listen and circle. Does it start with a?

1.	2.	3.	4.
✔ ✗	✔ ✗	✔ ✗	✔ ✗

Look and do.

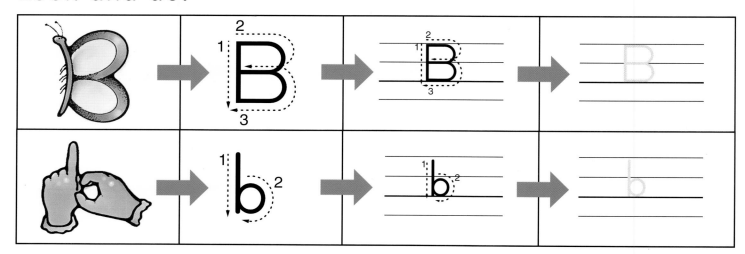

Write and say.

B

b

Listen and circle. Does it start with b?

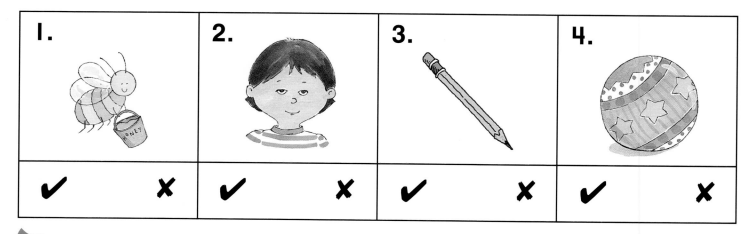

1.	2.	3.	4.
✔ ✘	✔ ✘	✔ ✘	✔ ✘

Cc Practice

Look and do.

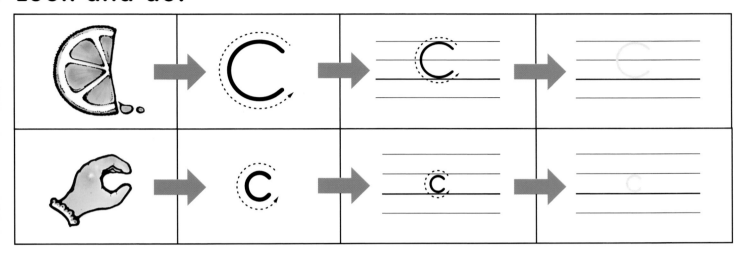

Write and say.

C   C

c   c

Listen and circle. Does it start with c?

1.	2.	3.	4.
✔ ✗	✔ ✗	✔ ✗	✔ ✗

Activities

Listen and sing.

ABC ABC If you know these, wink, wink, wink!

Listen and write the letters. Then say the word.

c _ _ _

Listen and circle the pictures.

Which words begin with b?	Which words begin with c?

Which words begin with b?

1.  2.

3.  4.

Which words begin with c?

1.  2.

3.  4.

8

Review

Put a sticker over the letters you know.

Aa   Bb   Cc

Point to the words you know.

Teacher's Comments

Story Time

Listen and point.

New Words

Listen to the chant. Then find the stickers.

Dd

Find another d word.

Ee
  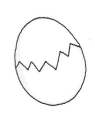

Find another e word.

Ff

Find another f word.

Now say the chant!

Dd Practice

Look and do.

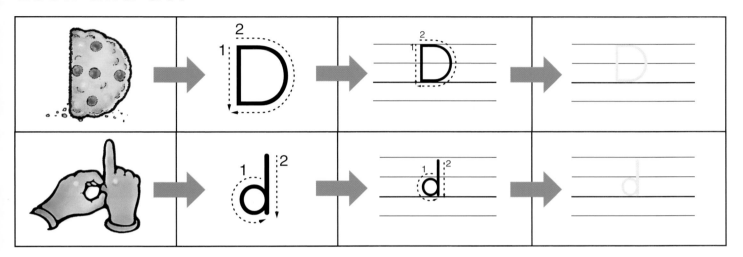

Write and say.

D

d

Listen and circle. Does it start with d?

1.	2.	3.	4.
✔ ✗	✔ ✗	✔ ✗	✔ ✗

13

Ee Practice

Look and do.

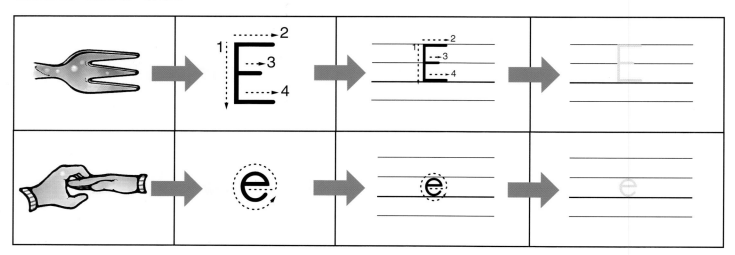

Write and say.

E   E

e   e

Listen and circle. Does it start with e?

1.	2.	3.	4.
✔ ✘	✔ ✘	✔ ✘	✔ ✘

Ff Practice

Look and do.

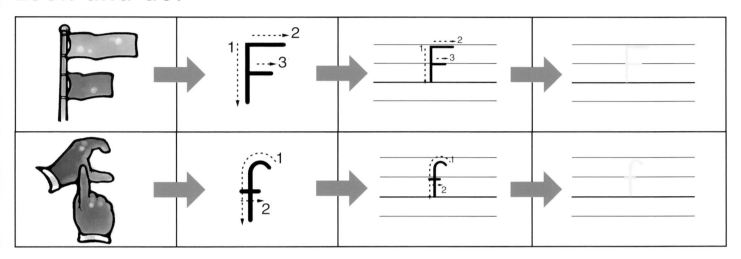

Write and say.

F

f

Listen and circle. Does it start with f?

1.	2.	3.	4.
5			
✔ ✗	✔ ✗	✔ ✗	✔ ✗

15

Activities

Listen and sing.

DEF DEF If you know these, wiggle, wiggle, wiggle!

Listen and write the missing a or e.

1. c _a_ p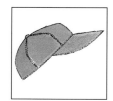

2. b __ d

3. p __ n

4. c __ t

Listen and circle the pictures.

Which words begin with d?	**Which words begin with f?**

1.    2.

1. 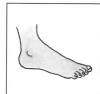   2.

3.    4.

3.    4.

Review

Put a sticker over the letters you know.

Dd　　Ee　　Ff

Point to the words you know.

 Teacher's Comments

Unit **3**

Story Time

Listen and point.

18

New Words

Listen to the chant. Then find the stickers.

G g

 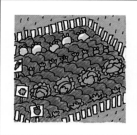 

Find another **g** word.

H h

Find another **h** word.

I i

Find another **i** word.

Now say the chant!

20

Gg Practice

Look and do.

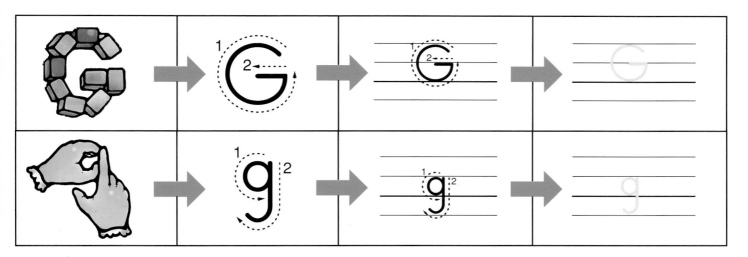

Write and say.

G G

g g

Listen and circle. Does it start with g?

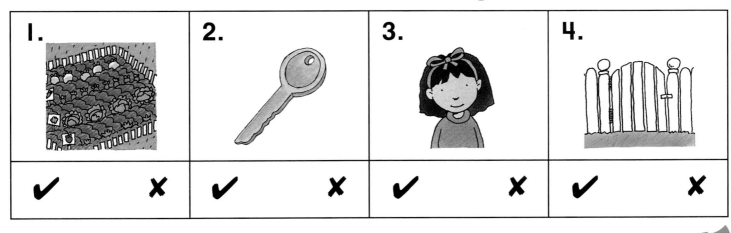

1.	2.	3.	4.
✔ ✗	✔ ✗	✔ ✗	✔ ✗

Hh Practice

Look and do.

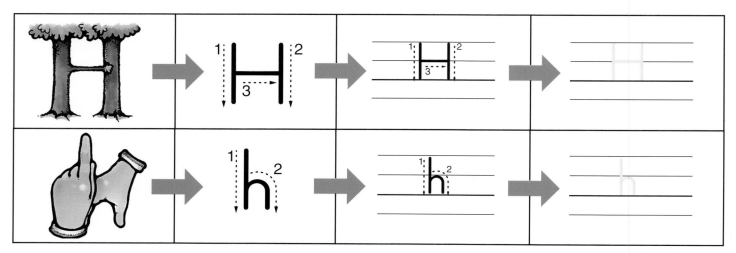

Write and say.

H

h

Listen and circle. Does it start with h?

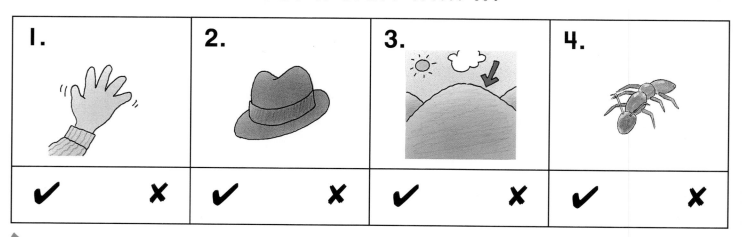

1.	2.	3.	4.
✔ ✗	✔ ✗	✔ ✗	✔ ✗

22

Ii Practice

Look and do.

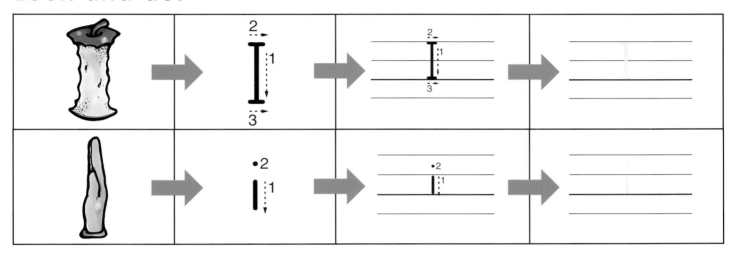

Write and say.

I

i

Listen and circle. Does it start with i?

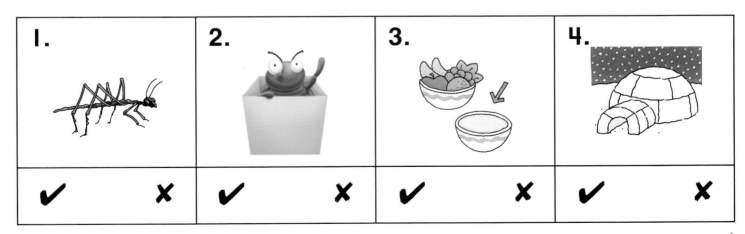

1.	2.	3.	4.
✔ ✗	✔ ✗	✔ ✗	✔ ✗

23

Activities

Listen and sing.

GHI GHI If you know these, clap, clap, clap!

Listen and write the missing a, e, or i.

1. b __ t

2. p __ n

3. s __ t

4. n __ t

Read the words aloud quickly. Then practice with the cassette.

bad	bed	big
bag	beg	did
dad	fed	fig
cab		hid

I read these words in _____ seconds.

24

Review

Put a sticker over the letters you know.

Gg   Hh   Ii

Point to the words you know.

Teacher's Comments

Story Time

Listen and point.

New Words

Listen to the chant. Then find the stickers.

J j

Find another **j** word.

K k

Find another **k** word.

L l

Find another **l** word.

Now say the chant!

28

J j Practice

Look and do.

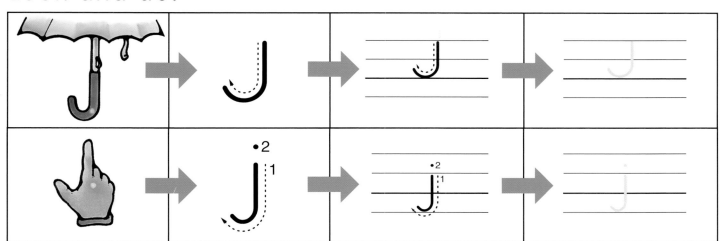

Write and say.

J J J

j j j

Listen and circle. Does it start with j?

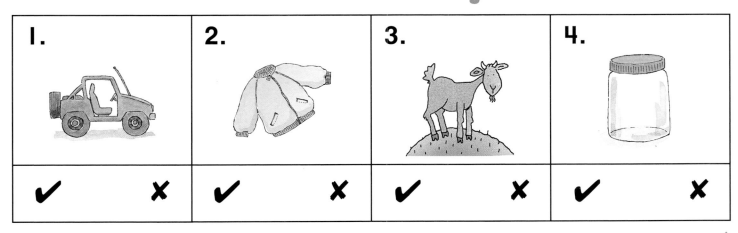

1.	2.	3.	4.
✔ ✗	✔ ✗	✔ ✗	✔ ✗

Kk Practice

Look and do.

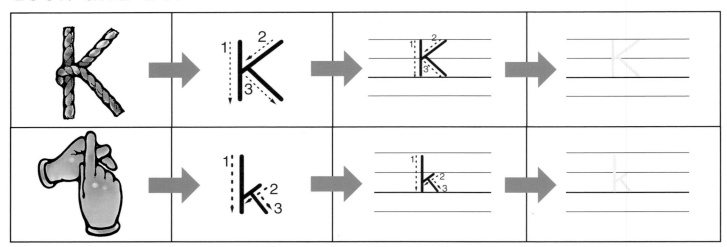

Write and say.

K K

k k

Listen and circle. Does it start with k?

1.	2.	3.	4.
✔ ✗	✔ ✗	✔ ✗	✔ ✗

30

Ll Practice

Look and do.

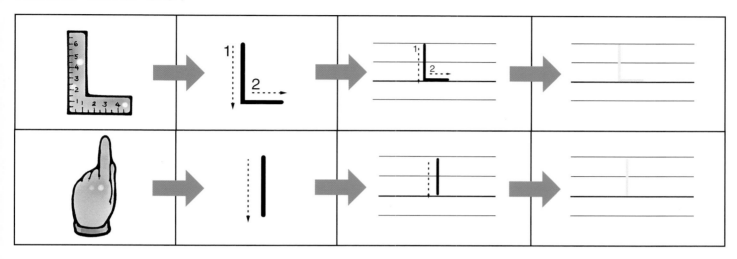

Write and say.

Listen and circle. Does it start with l?

1.	2.	3.	4.
✔ ✗	✔ ✗	✔ ✗	✔ ✗

Activities

Listen and sing.

JKL JKL If you know these, stomp, stomp, stomp!

Listen and circle the pictures.

Which words begin with j?

1.
2.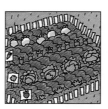
3.
4.

Which words begin with l?

1.
2.
3.
4.

Listen and write the missing g or k.

1. ___ite

2. ___oose

3. ___ey

4. ___itten

Review

Put a sticker over the letters you know.

Jj   Kk   Ll

Point to the words you know.

Teacher's Comments

Story Time

Listen and point.

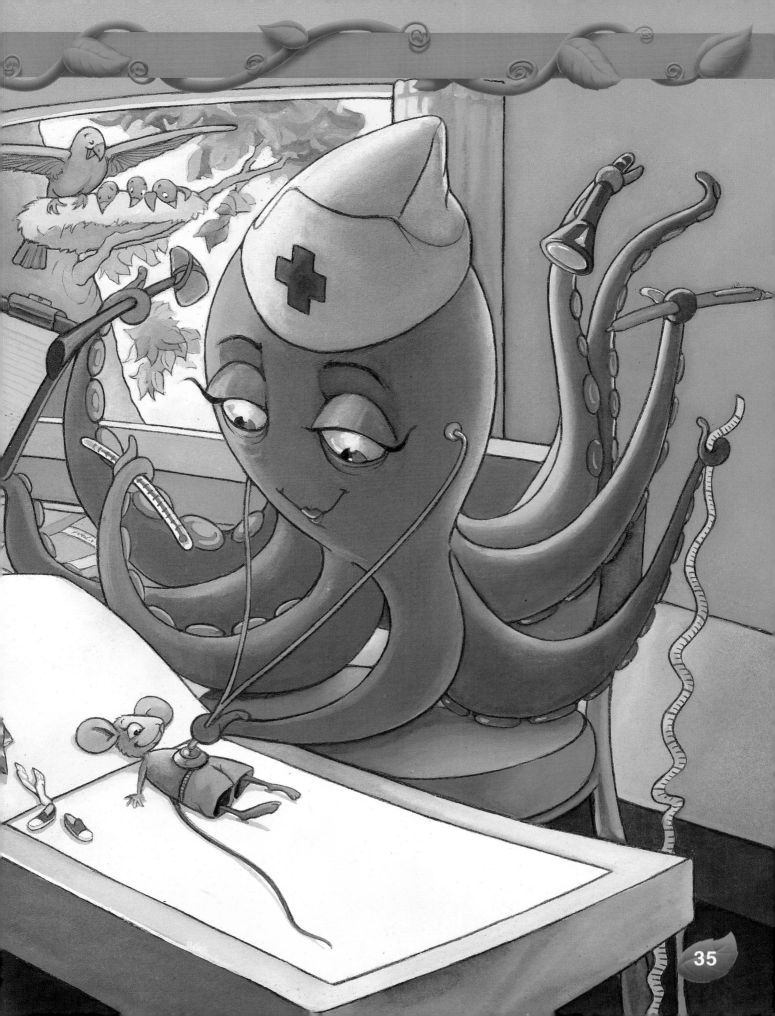

New Words

Listen to the chant. Then find the stickers.

Mm

Find another **m** word.

Nn

Find another **n** word.

Oo

Find another **o** word.

Now say the chant!

Mm Practice

Look and do.

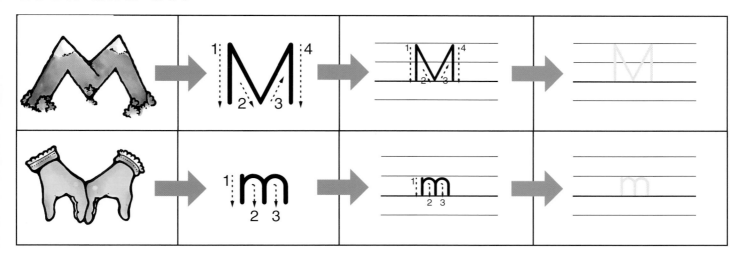

Write and say.

M   M

m   m

Listen and circle. Does it start with m?

1.	2.	3.	4.
✔ ✗	✔ ✗	✔ ✗	✔ ✗

Nn Practice

Look and do.

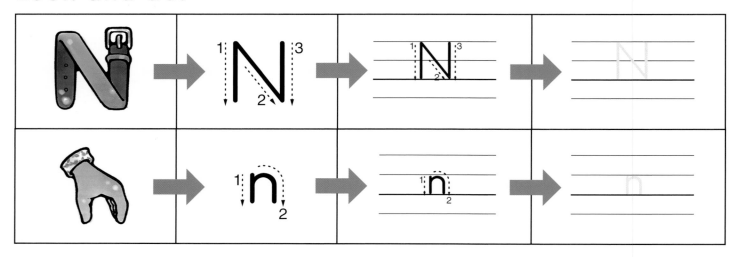

Write and say.

N N

n n

Listen and circle. Does it start with n?

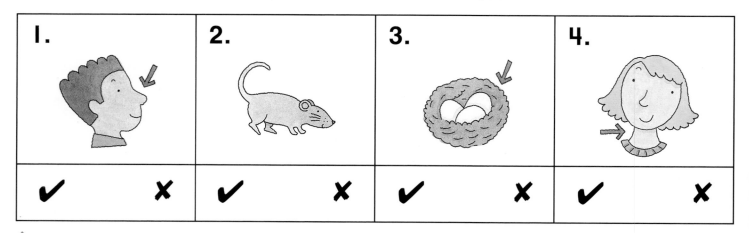

1. ✔ ✗
2. ✔ ✗
3. ✔ ✗
4. ✔ ✗

Oo Practice

Look and do.

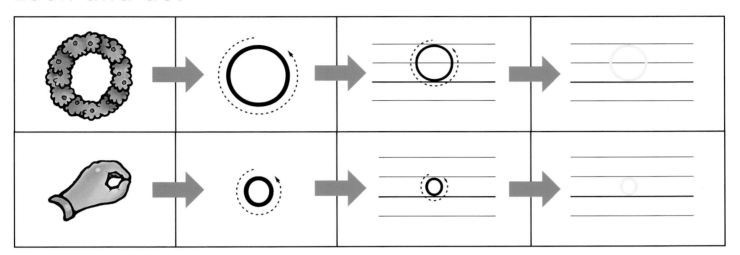

Write and say.

Listen and circle. Does it start with o?

1.	2.	3.	4.
✔ ✘	✔ ✘	✔ ✘	✔ ✘

Activities

Listen and sing.

MNO MNO   If you know these, wave, wave, wave!

Listen and write the missing m or n.

1. __ap

2. __ose

3. __ine

4. __ilk

Read the words aloud quickly. Then practice with the cassette.

mad
lag
had

leg
beg
hen

bid
dig
bib

nod
job
mom

I read these words in _____ seconds.

Review

Put a sticker over the letters you know.

Mm Nn Oo

Point to the words you know.

 **Teacher's Comments**

Story Time

Listen and point.

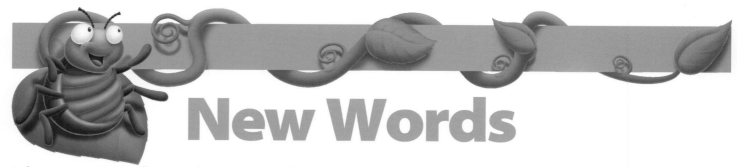

New Words

Listen to the chant. Then find the stickers.

Pp    Find another p word.

Qq    Find another q word.

Rr    Find another r word.

Now say the chant!

Pp Practice

Look and do.

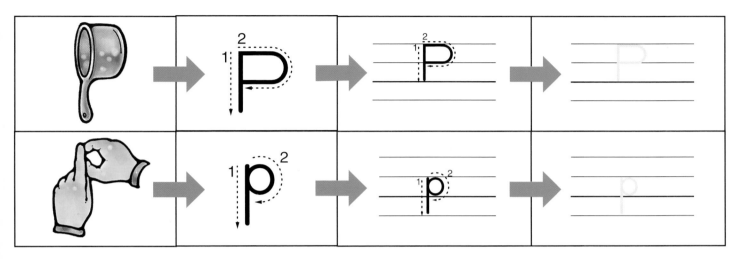

Write and say.

P P

p p

Listen and circle. Does it start with p?

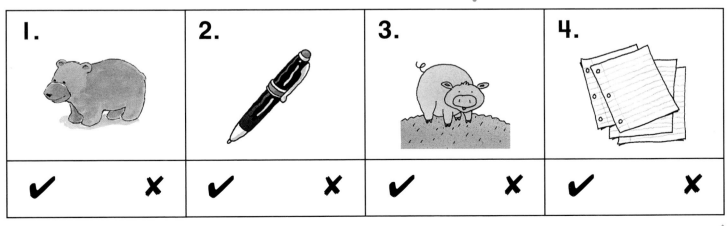

1.	2.	3.	4.
✔ ✗	✔ ✗	✔ ✗	✔ ✗

Qq Practice

Look and do.

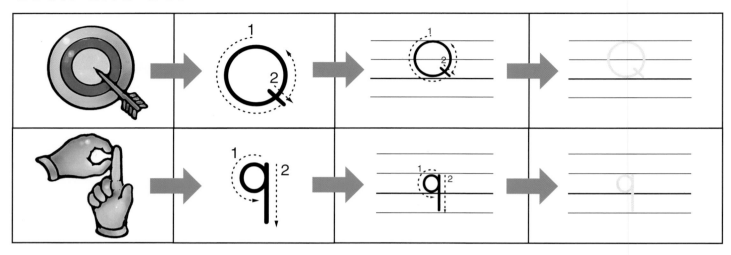

Write and say.

Q $\quad$ Q

q $\quad$ q

Listen and circle. Does it start with q?

1. ✔ ✗
2. ✔ ✗
3. ✔ ✗
4. ✔ ✗

Rr Practice

Look and do.

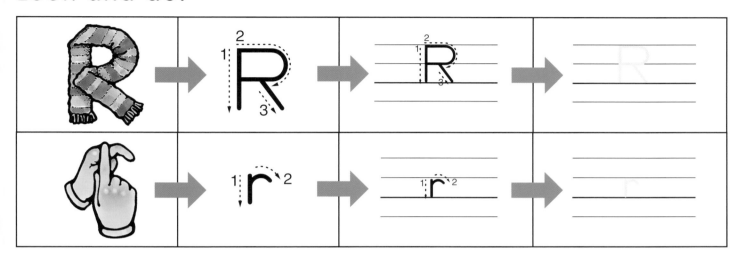

Write and say.

R

r

Listen and circle. Does it start with r?

1.	2.	3.	4.
✔ ✗	✔ ✗	✔ ✗	✔ ✗

47

Activities

Listen and sing.

PQR PQR If you know these, hop, hop, hop!

Listen and circle the pictures.

Which words begin with q?

1.  2.

3.  4.

Which words begin with r?

1.  2.

3.  4.

Read the words aloud quickly. Then practice with the cassette.

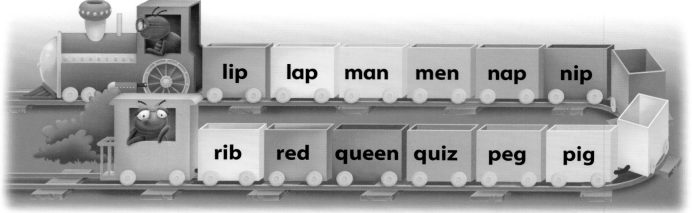

lip lap man men nap nip

rib red queen quiz peg pig

I read these words in _____ seconds.

Review

Put a sticker over the letters you know.

Pp   Qq   Rr

Point to the words you know.

Teacher's Comments

Story Time

Listen and point.

New Words

Listen to the chant. Then find the stickers.

Ss
   Find another **s** word.

Tt
   Find another **t** word.

Uu
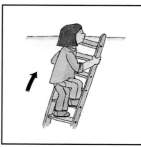   Find another **u** word.

Now say the chant!

Ss Practice

Look and do.

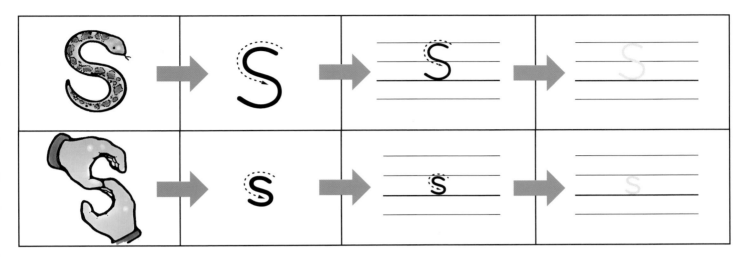

Write and say.

S

s

Listen and circle. Does it start with s?

1.	2.	3.	4.
✔ ✗	✔ ✗	✔ ✗	✔ ✗

Tt Practice

Look and do.

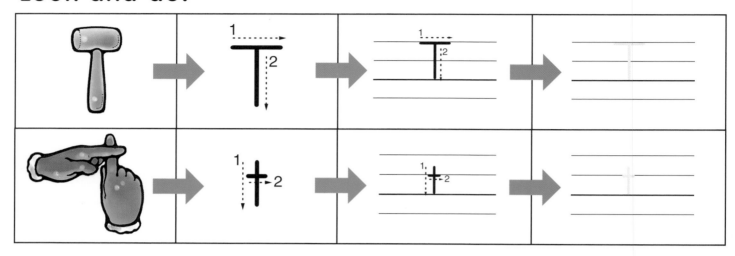

Write and say.

T

t

Listen and circle. Does it start with t?

1.   ✔   ✘
2.   ✔   ✘
3.   ✔   ✘
4.   ✔   ✘

Look and do.

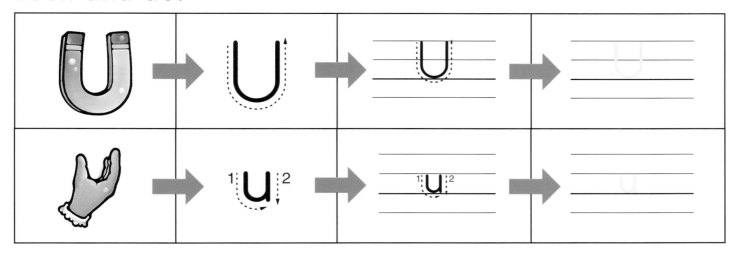

Write and say.

U

u

Listen and circle. Does it start with u?

1.	2.	3.	4.
✔ ✗	✔ ✗	✔ ✗	✔ ✗

Activities

Listen and sing.

STU STU If you know these, jump, jump, jump!

Listen and write the missing t or d.

1. __ape

2. __og

3. __axi

4. __oys

Read the words aloud quickly. Then practice with the cassette.

bus
bug
set
bud
cup
tan
hat
hot
tin
but
mud
sun
net
jet

I read these words in _____ seconds.

56

Review

Put a sticker over the letters you know.

Ss   Tt   Uu

Point to the words you know.

Teacher's Comments

Listen and point.

New Words

Listen to the chant. Then find the stickers.

Vv    Find another **v** word.

Ww    Find another **w** word.

Xx   Find another word that ends in **x**.

Now say the chant!

Vv Practice

Look and do.

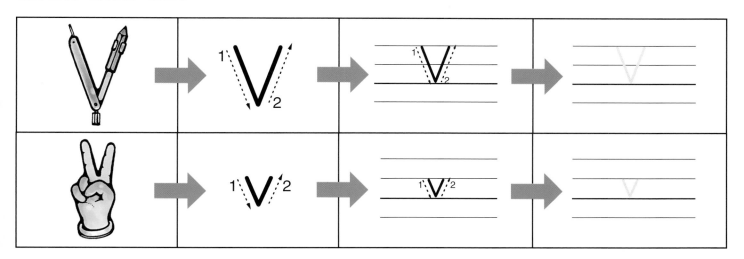

Write and say.

V

V

Listen and circle. Does it start with v?

1.	2.	3.	4.
✔ ✘	✔ ✘	✔ ✘	✔ ✘

Ww Practice

Look and do.

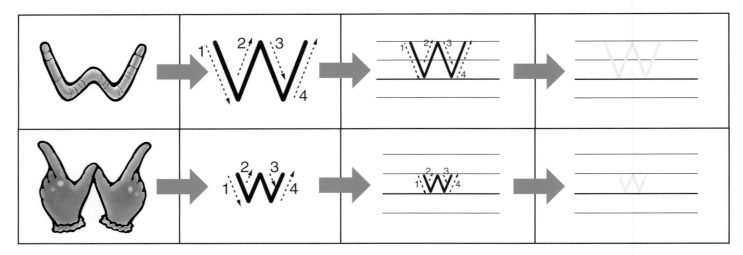

Write and say.

W W

W W

Listen and circle. Does it start with w?

1.	2.	3.	4.
✔ ✗	✔ ✗	✔ ✗	✔ ✗

Xx Practice

Look and do.

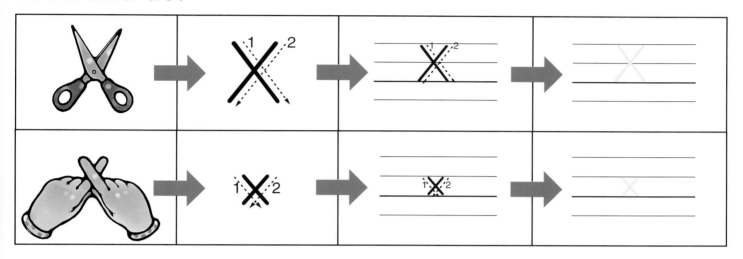

Write and say.

X   X

X   X

Listen and circle. Does it end with x?

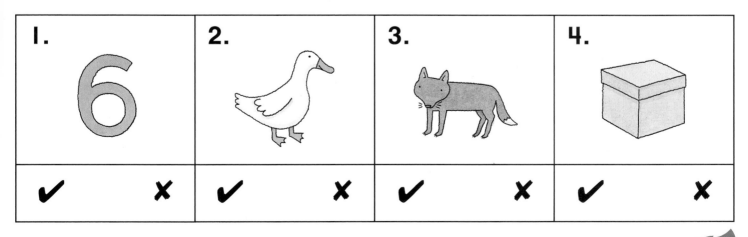

1.	2.	3.	4.
✔ ✘	✔ ✘	✔ ✘	✔ ✘

Activities

Listen and sing.

VWX VWX If you know these, shout, shout, shout!

Listen and write the missing f or v.

1. ___an

2. ___oot
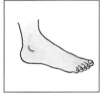

3. ___iolin

4. ___ive

Read the words aloud quickly. Then practice with the cassette.

box
fox
vat

fix
lip
win

wig
sad
lid

rid
fax
mix

hut
wax
tax

I read these words in _____ seconds.

64

Review

Put a sticker over the letters you know.

Vv Ww Xx

Point to the words you know.

Story Time

Listen and point.

New Words

Listen to the chant. Then find the stickers.

Yy

Find another **y** word.

Zz

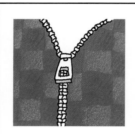

Find another **z** word.

Now say the chant!

68

Yy Practice

Look and do.

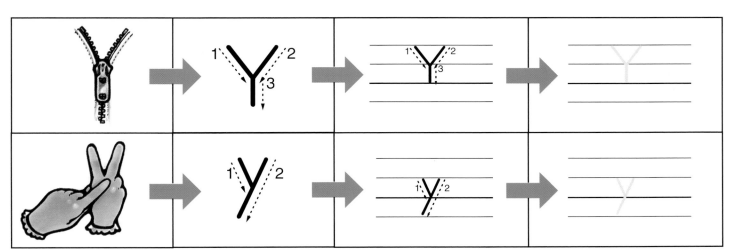

Write and say.

Y Y

Y Y

Listen and circle. Does it start with y?

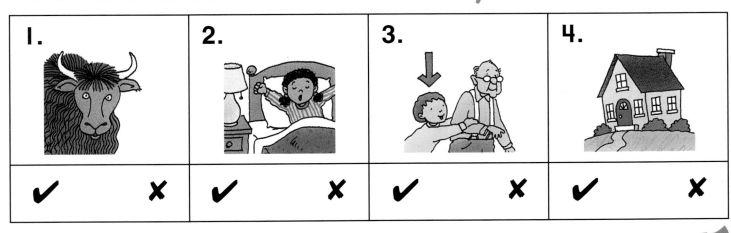

1. ✔ ✗

2. ✔ ✗

3. ✔ ✗

4. ✔ ✗

69

Zz Practice

Look and do.

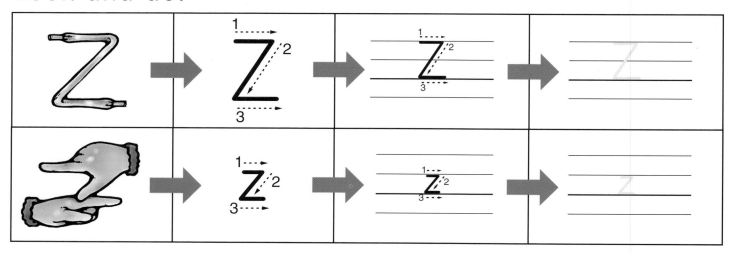

Write and say.

Z z

z z

Listen and circle. Does it start with z?

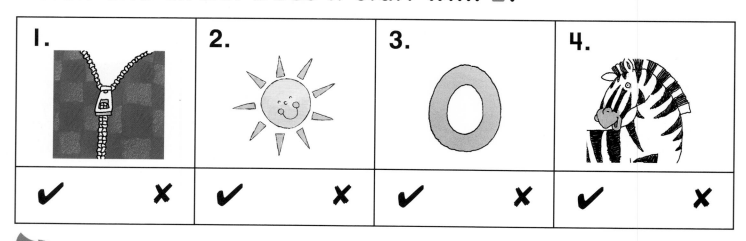

1.	2.	3.	4.
✔ ✗	✔ ✗	✔ ✗	✔ ✗

70

Activities

Listen and sing.

Y and Z, Y and Z If you know these, give me five!

Listen and write the missing s or z.

1. ___ebra

2. ___ister

3. ___ipper

4. ___even

Read the words aloud quickly. Then practice with the cassette.

wet yes rat

sit fox red

wig zip leg

web yes lid

six den box

let zap get

 I read these words in _____ seconds.

Review

Put a sticker over the letters you know.

Yy   Zz

Point to the words you know.

 Teacher's Comments

Sing it all together!

ABC, ABC, If you know these, wink, wink, wink!

DEF, DEF, If you know these, wiggle, wiggle, wiggle!

GHI, GHI, If you know these, clap, clap, clap!

JKL, JKL, If you know these, stomp, stomp, stomp!

MNO, MNO, If you know these, wave, wave, wave!

PQR, PQR, If you know these, hop, hop, hop!

STU, STU, If you know these, jump, jump, jump!

VWX, VWX, If you know these, shout, shout, shout!

Y and Z, Y and Z, If you know these, give me five!

Vocabulary Review

 ax
 apple
 animals
 ant

 bee
 boy
 bear
 ball

 cake
 cap
 cook
 cat

 donkey
 duck
 door
 dog

 elephant
 empty
 egg
 elbow

 fish
 fan
 face
 five

 goat
 garden
 gate
 girl

 house
 hand
 hat
 hill

ink   insect   in   igloo

jar   jacket   juice   jeep

kitten   key   kitchen   kite

leg   lake   lion   lamp

mouse   mother   map   monkey

nurse   nose   nest   neck

ostrich   octopus   on   October

pig   pencil   paper   pen

quilt   quiz   question   queen

red

 run

 rain

 rabbit

 sun

 sea

 sit

 saw

 tent

 telephone

 teacher

 taxi

 up

 uncle

 under

 umbrella

 vest

 vase

 violin

 vegetables

 watch

 wet

 window

 water

 fox

 six

 ox

 box

 yacht

 yawn

 young

 yak

 zoo

 zipper

 zero

 zebra

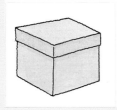   

Ss	Nn	Cc	Uu
Ll	Ff	Rr	Bb
Zz	Aa	Kk	Oo
Mm	Ee	Ww	Pp
Yy	Ii	Gg	Tt
Qq	Vv	Dd	Xx
Jj	Hh		